50 The Ultimate Pancake & Waffle Cookbook Recipes

By: Kelly Johnson

Table of Contents

- Classic Buttermilk Pancakes
- Fluffy Japanese Soufflé Pancakes
- Blueberry Lemon Pancakes
- Chocolate Chip Pancakes
- Banana Walnut Pancakes
- Pumpkin Spice Pancakes
- Peanut Butter & Jelly Pancakes
- Red Velvet Pancakes with Cream Cheese Drizzle
- Cinnamon Roll Pancakes
- Oatmeal Raisin Pancakes
- Carrot Cake Pancakes
- Apple Cinnamon Pancakes
- Matcha Green Tea Pancakes
- Mocha Espresso Pancakes
- Almond Flour Keto Pancakes
- Gingerbread Pancakes
- Piña Colada Pancakes (Pineapple & Coconut)
- Strawberry Shortcake Pancakes
- Protein Pancakes (Greek Yogurt & Oats)
- Chocolate Hazelnut Pancakes
- Sweet Potato Pancakes
- Churro Pancakes with Cinnamon Sugar
- Lemon Poppy Seed Pancakes
- Raspberry White Chocolate Pancakes
- Tiramisu Pancakes
- Classic Belgian Waffles
- Buttermilk Waffles
- Chocolate Brownie Waffles
- Banana Bread Waffles
- Pumpkin Spice Waffles
- Cheddar & Chive Savory Waffles
- Cinnamon Sugar Churro Waffles
- Strawberry & Cream Waffles
- Lemon Ricotta Waffles
- Matcha Mochi Waffles

- Red Velvet Waffles
- Peanut Butter Banana Waffles
- S'mores Waffles with Marshmallow Drizzle
- Maple Bacon Waffles
- Apple Cider Waffles
- Carrot Cake Waffles with Cream Cheese Glaze
- Coconut Flour Keto Waffles
- Blueberry Cornmeal Waffles
- Gingerbread Waffles
- Taro Ube Waffles
- Mocha Espresso Waffles
- Bourbon Pecan Waffles
- Honey Butter Sweet Potato Waffles
- Raspberry Almond Waffles
- Chocolate-Stuffed Waffles

Classic Buttermilk Pancakes

Ingredients:

- 1 ½ cups all-purpose flour
- 1 tbsp sugar
- 1 tsp baking powder
- ½ tsp baking soda
- ¼ tsp salt
- 1 ¼ cups buttermilk
- 1 egg
- 2 tbsp melted butter
- 1 tsp vanilla extract

Instructions:

1. **Prepare batter** – In a bowl, whisk together flour, sugar, baking powder, baking soda, and salt.
2. **Mix wet ingredients** – In another bowl, whisk buttermilk, egg, melted butter, and vanilla.
3. **Combine** – Gradually mix wet ingredients into the dry, stirring until just combined.
4. **Cook pancakes** – Heat a griddle over medium heat and pour ¼ cup of batter per pancake. Cook until bubbles form, then flip and cook for another minute.
5. **Serve** – Serve warm with butter and maple syrup.

Fluffy Japanese Soufflé Pancakes

Ingredients:

- 2 eggs, separated
- 2 tbsp sugar
- ½ cup all-purpose flour
- ½ tsp baking powder
- ¼ cup milk
- ½ tsp vanilla extract
- ½ tsp cream of tartar
- 1 tbsp butter (for cooking)

Instructions:

1. **Make batter** – Whisk egg yolks, sugar, milk, and vanilla. Sift in flour and baking powder, then mix gently.
2. **Whip egg whites** – Beat egg whites with cream of tartar until stiff peaks form.
3. **Fold together** – Gently fold egg whites into the batter.
4. **Cook pancakes** – Heat a nonstick pan on low, grease with butter, and spoon tall portions of batter onto the pan. Cover and cook for 4–5 minutes per side.
5. **Serve** – Serve with powdered sugar, fruit, or syrup.

Blueberry Lemon Pancakes

Ingredients:

- 1 ½ cups all-purpose flour
- 1 tbsp sugar
- 1 tsp baking powder
- ½ tsp baking soda
- ¼ tsp salt
- 1 ¼ cups buttermilk
- 1 egg
- 1 tbsp lemon zest
- 1 tsp vanilla extract
- ¾ cup fresh blueberries

Instructions:

1. **Prepare batter** – In a bowl, whisk together flour, sugar, baking powder, baking soda, and salt.
2. **Mix wet ingredients** – Whisk buttermilk, egg, lemon zest, and vanilla.
3. **Combine** – Stir wet ingredients into dry ingredients until just combined, then fold in blueberries.
4. **Cook pancakes** – Heat a griddle over medium heat and cook pancakes until golden brown.
5. **Serve** – Serve with syrup, butter, or extra blueberries.

Chocolate Chip Pancakes

Ingredients:

- 1 ½ cups all-purpose flour
- 1 tbsp sugar
- 1 tsp baking powder
- ½ tsp baking soda
- ¼ tsp salt
- 1 ¼ cups buttermilk
- 1 egg
- 1 tsp vanilla extract
- ¾ cup chocolate chips

Instructions:

1. **Prepare batter** – Mix dry ingredients in a bowl. In another bowl, whisk buttermilk, egg, and vanilla.
2. **Combine** – Stir wet ingredients into dry ingredients until just combined, then fold in chocolate chips.
3. **Cook pancakes** – Pour batter onto a heated griddle and cook until bubbles form, then flip and cook another minute.
4. **Serve** – Serve warm with butter, syrup, or extra chocolate chips.

Banana Walnut Pancakes

Ingredients:

- 1 ½ cups all-purpose flour
- 1 tbsp sugar
- 1 tsp baking powder
- ½ tsp baking soda
- ¼ tsp salt
- 1 ripe banana, mashed
- 1 ¼ cups buttermilk
- 1 egg
- 1 tsp vanilla extract
- ½ cup chopped walnuts

Instructions:

1. **Prepare batter** – Mix dry ingredients in a bowl. In another bowl, whisk mashed banana, buttermilk, egg, and vanilla.
2. **Combine** – Stir wet ingredients into dry, then fold in walnuts.
3. **Cook pancakes** – Cook on a medium-heat griddle until golden.
4. **Serve** – Serve with maple syrup and extra walnuts.

Pumpkin Spice Pancakes

Ingredients:

- 1 ½ cups all-purpose flour
- 1 tbsp sugar
- 1 tsp baking powder
- ½ tsp baking soda
- ½ tsp cinnamon
- ½ tsp pumpkin spice
- ¼ tsp salt
- 1 cup pumpkin puree
- 1 cup buttermilk
- 1 egg
- 1 tsp vanilla extract

Instructions:

1. **Prepare batter** – Mix dry ingredients in a bowl. In another bowl, whisk pumpkin puree, buttermilk, egg, and vanilla.
2. **Combine** – Stir wet ingredients into dry ingredients until just combined.
3. **Cook pancakes** – Pour batter onto a hot griddle and cook until golden.
4. **Serve** – Serve with whipped cream, syrup, or cinnamon sugar.

Peanut Butter & Jelly Pancakes

Ingredients:

- 1 ½ cups all-purpose flour
- 1 tbsp sugar
- 1 tsp baking powder
- ½ tsp baking soda
- ¼ tsp salt
- 1 ¼ cups buttermilk
- 1 egg
- 1 tsp vanilla extract
- ¼ cup peanut butter
- ¼ cup fruit jam

Instructions:

1. **Prepare batter** – Mix dry ingredients in a bowl. In another bowl, whisk buttermilk, egg, vanilla, and peanut butter.
2. **Combine** – Stir wet ingredients into dry ingredients.
3. **Cook pancakes** – Pour batter onto a heated griddle and cook until golden.
4. **Serve** – Drizzle pancakes with warm jam and top with peanut butter.

Red Velvet Pancakes with Cream Cheese Drizzle

Ingredients:

- 1 ½ cups all-purpose flour
- 1 tbsp cocoa powder
- 1 tbsp sugar
- 1 tsp baking powder
- ½ tsp baking soda
- ¼ tsp salt
- 1 cup buttermilk
- 1 egg
- 1 tsp vanilla extract
- 1 tbsp red food coloring

For Cream Cheese Drizzle:

- 2 oz cream cheese, softened
- ¼ cup powdered sugar
- 1 tbsp milk
- ½ tsp vanilla extract

Instructions:

1. **Prepare batter** – Mix dry ingredients in a bowl. In another bowl, whisk buttermilk, egg, vanilla, and red food coloring.
2. **Combine** – Stir wet ingredients into dry ingredients until just combined.
3. **Cook pancakes** – Pour batter onto a hot griddle and cook until golden.
4. **Make drizzle** – Whisk cream cheese, powdered sugar, milk, and vanilla until smooth.
5. **Serve** – Drizzle cream cheese topping over warm pancakes.

Cinnamon Roll Pancakes

Ingredients:

For Pancakes:

- 1 ½ cups all-purpose flour
- 1 tbsp sugar
- 1 tsp baking powder
- ½ tsp baking soda
- ¼ tsp salt
- 1 ¼ cups buttermilk
- 1 egg
- 1 tsp vanilla extract

For Cinnamon Swirl:

- ¼ cup melted butter
- ¼ cup brown sugar
- 1 tsp cinnamon

For Cream Cheese Glaze:

- 2 oz cream cheese, softened
- ¼ cup powdered sugar
- 1 tbsp milk
- ½ tsp vanilla extract

Instructions:

1. **Prepare cinnamon swirl** – Mix melted butter, brown sugar, and cinnamon in a small bowl. Transfer to a piping bag.
2. **Prepare pancake batter** – Whisk together dry ingredients, then stir in buttermilk, egg, and vanilla.
3. **Cook pancakes** – Pour batter onto a hot griddle. Pipe a cinnamon swirl into the batter. Flip and cook.
4. **Make glaze** – Mix cream cheese, powdered sugar, milk, and vanilla until smooth.
5. **Serve** – Drizzle pancakes with cream cheese glaze and enjoy.

Oatmeal Raisin Pancakes

Ingredients:

- 1 cup oats, blended into flour
- ½ cup whole wheat flour
- 1 tbsp sugar
- 1 tsp cinnamon
- 1 tsp baking powder
- ½ tsp baking soda
- ¼ tsp salt
- 1 cup buttermilk
- 1 egg
- ½ tsp vanilla extract
- ¼ cup raisins

Instructions:

1. **Prepare batter** – Mix dry ingredients in a bowl. In another bowl, whisk buttermilk, egg, and vanilla.
2. **Combine** – Stir wet ingredients into dry, then fold in raisins.
3. **Cook pancakes** – Pour batter onto a heated griddle and cook until golden brown.
4. **Serve** – Serve warm with butter and maple syrup.

Carrot Cake Pancakes

Ingredients:

- 1 ½ cups all-purpose flour
- 1 tbsp sugar
- 1 tsp baking powder
- ½ tsp baking soda
- 1 tsp cinnamon
- ½ tsp nutmeg
- ¼ tsp salt
- 1 cup buttermilk
- 1 egg
- 1 tsp vanilla extract
- ½ cup grated carrots
- ¼ cup chopped walnuts (optional)

Instructions:

1. **Prepare batter** – Mix dry ingredients. In another bowl, whisk buttermilk, egg, and vanilla.
2. **Combine** – Stir wet ingredients into dry, then fold in carrots and walnuts.
3. **Cook pancakes** – Pour batter onto a griddle and cook until golden.
4. **Serve** – Serve with maple syrup or cream cheese glaze.

Apple Cinnamon Pancakes

Ingredients:

- 1 ½ cups all-purpose flour
- 1 tbsp sugar
- 1 tsp baking powder
- ½ tsp baking soda
- 1 tsp cinnamon
- ¼ tsp salt
- 1 cup buttermilk
- 1 egg
- 1 tsp vanilla extract
- 1 cup grated apple

Instructions:

1. **Prepare batter** – Whisk together dry ingredients. In another bowl, mix buttermilk, egg, and vanilla.
2. **Combine** – Stir wet ingredients into dry, then fold in grated apple.
3. **Cook pancakes** – Cook on a medium-heat griddle until golden.
4. **Serve** – Serve with honey, syrup, or cinnamon sugar.

Matcha Green Tea Pancakes

Ingredients:

- 1 ½ cups all-purpose flour
- 1 tbsp sugar
- 1 tsp baking powder
- ½ tsp baking soda
- 1 tbsp matcha green tea powder
- ¼ tsp salt
- 1 cup buttermilk
- 1 egg
- 1 tsp vanilla extract

Instructions:

1. **Prepare batter** – Mix dry ingredients in a bowl. In another bowl, whisk buttermilk, egg, and vanilla.
2. **Combine** – Stir wet ingredients into dry until just combined.
3. **Cook pancakes** – Pour batter onto a heated griddle and cook until golden.
4. **Serve** – Serve with whipped cream and a dusting of matcha powder.

Mocha Espresso Pancakes

Ingredients:

- 1 ½ cups all-purpose flour
- 1 tbsp cocoa powder
- 1 tbsp sugar
- 1 tsp baking powder
- ½ tsp baking soda
- 1 tsp instant espresso powder
- ¼ tsp salt
- 1 cup buttermilk
- 1 egg
- 1 tsp vanilla extract

Instructions:

1. **Prepare batter** – Mix dry ingredients in a bowl. In another bowl, whisk buttermilk, egg, and vanilla.
2. **Combine** – Stir wet ingredients into dry ingredients.
3. **Cook pancakes** – Pour batter onto a griddle and cook until golden.
4. **Serve** – Top with chocolate syrup or whipped cream.

Almond Flour Keto Pancakes

Ingredients:

- 1 cup almond flour
- 1 tsp baking powder
- 1 tbsp sweetener (erythritol or monk fruit)
- ¼ tsp salt
- 2 eggs
- ¼ cup unsweetened almond milk
- 1 tsp vanilla extract

Instructions:

1. **Prepare batter** – Mix dry ingredients. In another bowl, whisk eggs, almond milk, and vanilla.
2. **Combine** – Stir wet ingredients into dry until smooth.
3. **Cook pancakes** – Pour batter onto a griddle and cook on low heat.
4. **Serve** – Serve with sugar-free syrup or fresh berries.

Gingerbread Pancakes

Ingredients:

- 1 ½ cups all-purpose flour
- 1 tbsp brown sugar
- 1 tsp baking powder
- ½ tsp baking soda
- 1 tsp ground ginger
- ½ tsp cinnamon
- ¼ tsp nutmeg
- ¼ tsp salt
- 1 cup buttermilk
- 1 egg
- 1 tsp vanilla extract
- 2 tbsp molasses

Instructions:

1. **Prepare batter** – Mix dry ingredients. In another bowl, whisk buttermilk, egg, vanilla, and molasses.
2. **Combine** – Stir wet ingredients into dry until just combined.
3. **Cook pancakes** – Cook on a medium-heat griddle until golden.
4. **Serve** – Serve with whipped cream and maple syrup.

Piña Colada Pancakes (Pineapple & Coconut)

Ingredients:

- 1 ½ cups all-purpose flour
- 1 tbsp sugar
- 1 tsp baking powder
- ½ tsp baking soda
- ¼ tsp salt
- 1 cup coconut milk
- 1 egg
- 1 tsp vanilla extract
- ½ cup crushed pineapple, drained
- ¼ cup shredded coconut

Instructions:

1. **Prepare batter** – Mix dry ingredients. In another bowl, whisk coconut milk, egg, and vanilla.
2. **Combine** – Stir wet ingredients into dry, then fold in pineapple and coconut.
3. **Cook pancakes** – Pour batter onto a griddle and cook until golden.
4. **Serve** – Top with whipped cream and toasted coconut flakes.

Strawberry Shortcake Pancakes

Ingredients:

For Pancakes:

- 1 ½ cups all-purpose flour
- 1 tbsp sugar
- 1 tsp baking powder
- ½ tsp baking soda
- ¼ tsp salt
- 1 ¼ cups buttermilk
- 1 egg
- 1 tsp vanilla extract

For Topping:

- 1 cup fresh strawberries, sliced
- ½ cup whipped cream
- 1 tbsp powdered sugar

Instructions:

1. **Prepare batter** – Whisk dry ingredients in one bowl. In another bowl, mix buttermilk, egg, and vanilla.
2. **Combine** – Stir wet ingredients into dry until just combined.
3. **Cook pancakes** – Pour batter onto a griddle and cook until golden brown.
4. **Assemble** – Layer pancakes with fresh strawberries and whipped cream.
5. **Serve** – Sprinkle with powdered sugar and enjoy!

Protein Pancakes (Greek Yogurt & Oats)

Ingredients:

- ½ cup oats (blended into flour)
- ½ cup Greek yogurt
- 2 eggs
- 1 tsp vanilla extract
- 1 tsp baking powder
- ¼ tsp cinnamon
- 1 tbsp honey or maple syrup

Instructions:

1. **Blend oats** – Pulse oats into a fine flour.
2. **Prepare batter** – Mix oats with Greek yogurt, eggs, vanilla, baking powder, cinnamon, and honey.
3. **Cook pancakes** – Pour batter onto a griddle and cook on medium heat.
4. **Serve** – Serve with fresh fruit and a drizzle of honey.

Chocolate Hazelnut Pancakes

Ingredients:

- 1 ½ cups all-purpose flour
- 1 tbsp cocoa powder
- 1 tbsp sugar
- 1 tsp baking powder
- ½ tsp baking soda
- ¼ tsp salt
- 1 ¼ cups buttermilk
- 1 egg
- ¼ cup chocolate hazelnut spread (like Nutella)
- ¼ cup chopped hazelnuts

Instructions:

1. **Prepare batter** – Mix dry ingredients in one bowl. In another, whisk buttermilk, egg, and chocolate hazelnut spread.
2. **Combine** – Stir wet ingredients into dry until smooth.
3. **Cook pancakes** – Cook on a griddle until golden.
4. **Serve** – Top with extra hazelnut spread and chopped hazelnuts.

Sweet Potato Pancakes

Ingredients:

- 1 cup mashed sweet potato
- 1 cup all-purpose flour
- 1 tbsp sugar
- 1 tsp cinnamon
- 1 tsp baking powder
- ½ tsp baking soda
- ¼ tsp salt
- 1 cup buttermilk
- 1 egg
- 1 tsp vanilla extract

Instructions:

1. **Prepare batter** – Whisk dry ingredients. In another bowl, mix sweet potato, buttermilk, egg, and vanilla.
2. **Combine** – Stir wet ingredients into dry until just mixed.
3. **Cook pancakes** – Pour batter onto a griddle and cook until golden.
4. **Serve** – Serve with maple syrup and toasted pecans.

Churro Pancakes with Cinnamon Sugar

Ingredients:

For Pancakes:

- 1 ½ cups all-purpose flour
- 1 tbsp sugar
- 1 tsp cinnamon
- 1 tsp baking powder
- ½ tsp baking soda
- ¼ tsp salt
- 1 ¼ cups buttermilk
- 1 egg
- 1 tsp vanilla extract

For Topping:

- ¼ cup sugar
- 1 tsp cinnamon
- 2 tbsp melted butter

Instructions:

1. **Prepare batter** – Mix dry ingredients, then whisk in wet ingredients.
2. **Cook pancakes** – Pour batter onto a griddle and cook until golden.
3. **Coat pancakes** – Brush pancakes with melted butter, then sprinkle cinnamon sugar on top.
4. **Serve** – Serve warm with whipped cream or dulce de leche.

Lemon Poppy Seed Pancakes

Ingredients:

- 1 ½ cups all-purpose flour
- 1 tbsp sugar
- 1 tsp baking powder
- ½ tsp baking soda
- ¼ tsp salt
- 1 tbsp poppy seeds
- 1 tbsp lemon zest
- 1 cup buttermilk
- 1 egg
- 1 tsp vanilla extract

Instructions:

1. **Prepare batter** – Mix dry ingredients, then add wet ingredients and mix gently.
2. **Cook pancakes** – Pour batter onto a griddle and cook until golden.
3. **Serve** – Serve with lemon curd or powdered sugar.

Raspberry White Chocolate Pancakes

Ingredients:

- 1 ½ cups all-purpose flour
- 1 tbsp sugar
- 1 tsp baking powder
- ½ tsp baking soda
- ¼ tsp salt
- 1 ¼ cups buttermilk
- 1 egg
- ½ cup fresh raspberries
- ¼ cup white chocolate chips

Instructions:

1. **Prepare batter** – Whisk dry ingredients, then mix in wet ingredients until combined.
2. **Add mix-ins** – Fold in raspberries and white chocolate chips.
3. **Cook pancakes** – Pour batter onto a griddle and cook until golden.
4. **Serve** – Serve with syrup and extra raspberries.

Tiramisu Pancakes

Ingredients:

For Pancakes:

- 1 ½ cups all-purpose flour
- 1 tbsp cocoa powder
- 1 tbsp sugar
- 1 tsp baking powder
- ½ tsp baking soda
- ¼ tsp salt
- 1 cup buttermilk
- 1 egg
- 1 tsp espresso powder
- 1 tsp vanilla extract

For Mascarpone Topping:

- ½ cup mascarpone cheese
- 2 tbsp powdered sugar
- 1 tsp vanilla extract

Instructions:

1. **Prepare batter** – Mix dry ingredients, then stir in wet ingredients.
2. **Cook pancakes** – Cook on a griddle until golden.
3. **Make topping** – Whisk mascarpone, powdered sugar, and vanilla.
4. **Serve** – Spread mascarpone mixture between pancake layers, dust with cocoa powder, and serve.

Classic Belgian Waffles

Ingredients:

- 2 cups all-purpose flour
- 2 tbsp sugar
- 1 tbsp baking powder
- ½ tsp salt
- 2 eggs, separated
- 1 ¾ cups milk
- ½ cup melted butter
- 1 tsp vanilla extract

Instructions:

1. **Prepare dry ingredients** – Mix flour, sugar, baking powder, and salt in a bowl.
2. **Whisk wet ingredients** – Separate eggs, then mix yolks with milk, butter, and vanilla.
3. **Make batter** – Stir wet into dry, then fold in whipped egg whites for extra fluffiness.
4. **Cook waffles** – Pour batter into a preheated waffle iron and cook until crispy.
5. **Serve** – Serve with syrup, fruit, or whipped cream.

Buttermilk Waffles

Ingredients:

- 2 cups all-purpose flour
- 2 tbsp sugar
- 1 tbsp baking powder
- ½ tsp baking soda
- ½ tsp salt
- 2 eggs
- 1 ¾ cups buttermilk
- ½ cup melted butter
- 1 tsp vanilla extract

Instructions:

1. **Prepare dry ingredients** – In a large bowl, whisk together flour, sugar, baking powder, baking soda, and salt.
2. **Mix wet ingredients** – In a separate bowl, whisk eggs, buttermilk, melted butter, and vanilla.
3. **Combine** – Stir wet ingredients into dry ingredients until just combined.
4. **Cook waffles** – Pour batter into a preheated waffle iron and cook until golden brown.
5. **Serve** – Serve warm with butter and maple syrup.

Chocolate Brownie Waffles

Ingredients:

- 1 ½ cups all-purpose flour
- ½ cup cocoa powder
- ½ cup sugar
- 1 tbsp baking powder
- ¼ tsp salt
- 2 eggs
- 1 ½ cups milk
- ½ cup melted butter
- 1 tsp vanilla extract
- ½ cup chocolate chips

Instructions:

1. **Prepare batter** – Whisk dry ingredients in one bowl and wet ingredients in another.
2. **Combine** – Mix wet into dry ingredients, then fold in chocolate chips.
3. **Cook waffles** – Pour batter into a waffle iron and cook until crisp.
4. **Serve** – Serve with whipped cream, chocolate syrup, or powdered sugar.

Banana Bread Waffles

Ingredients:

- 1 ½ cups all-purpose flour
- 1 tbsp brown sugar
- 1 tsp baking powder
- ½ tsp baking soda
- ¼ tsp salt
- 1 tsp cinnamon
- 2 ripe bananas, mashed
- 2 eggs
- 1 cup milk
- ¼ cup melted butter
- 1 tsp vanilla extract
- ½ cup chopped walnuts (optional)

Instructions:

1. **Prepare batter** – Mix dry ingredients in one bowl. In another, whisk bananas, eggs, milk, butter, and vanilla.
2. **Combine** – Stir wet ingredients into dry, then fold in walnuts if using.
3. **Cook waffles** – Cook in a preheated waffle iron until golden brown.
4. **Serve** – Serve with maple syrup, extra bananas, and walnuts.

Pumpkin Spice Waffles

Ingredients:

- 1 ¾ cups all-purpose flour
- 1 tbsp sugar
- 1 tsp baking powder
- ½ tsp baking soda
- 1 tsp cinnamon
- ½ tsp nutmeg
- ¼ tsp ginger
- ¼ tsp salt
- 1 cup pumpkin puree
- 2 eggs
- 1 ½ cups milk
- ¼ cup melted butter
- 1 tsp vanilla extract

Instructions:

1. **Prepare batter** – Mix dry ingredients in one bowl. In another, whisk pumpkin, eggs, milk, butter, and vanilla.
2. **Combine** – Stir wet ingredients into dry until smooth.
3. **Cook waffles** – Cook in a preheated waffle iron until golden brown.
4. **Serve** – Serve with whipped cream and a sprinkle of cinnamon sugar.

Cheddar & Chive Savory Waffles

Ingredients:

- 1 ½ cups all-purpose flour
- 1 tsp baking powder
- ½ tsp baking soda
- ¼ tsp salt
- ½ tsp garlic powder
- 1 cup shredded cheddar cheese
- 2 tbsp chopped chives
- 2 eggs
- 1 ¼ cups buttermilk
- ¼ cup melted butter

Instructions:

1. **Prepare batter** – Whisk dry ingredients, then stir in cheddar and chives.
2. **Mix wet ingredients** – In another bowl, whisk eggs, buttermilk, and melted butter.
3. **Combine** – Stir wet ingredients into dry until just mixed.
4. **Cook waffles** – Cook in a waffle iron until crispy.
5. **Serve** – Serve with sour cream or a fried egg on top.

Cinnamon Sugar Churro Waffles

Ingredients:

For Waffles:

- 2 cups all-purpose flour
- 1 tbsp sugar
- 1 tbsp baking powder
- ½ tsp salt
- 1 ¾ cups milk
- 2 eggs
- ½ cup melted butter
- 1 tsp vanilla extract

For Topping:

- ½ cup sugar
- 1 tsp cinnamon
- ¼ cup melted butter

Instructions:

1. **Prepare batter** – Whisk dry and wet ingredients separately, then combine.
2. **Cook waffles** – Cook waffles in a preheated waffle iron until golden.
3. **Coat waffles** – Brush waffles with melted butter and sprinkle with cinnamon sugar.
4. **Serve** – Serve warm with chocolate sauce or caramel drizzle.

Strawberry & Cream Waffles

Ingredients:

- 2 cups all-purpose flour
- 1 tbsp sugar
- 1 tbsp baking powder
- ½ tsp salt
- 2 eggs
- 1 ¾ cups milk
- ½ cup melted butter
- 1 tsp vanilla extract
- 1 cup fresh strawberries, sliced

For Topping:

- ½ cup whipped cream
- 2 tbsp powdered sugar

Instructions:

1. **Prepare batter** – Mix dry ingredients. In another bowl, whisk eggs, milk, butter, and vanilla.
2. **Combine** – Stir wet ingredients into dry, then fold in strawberries.
3. **Cook waffles** – Cook in a preheated waffle iron until golden.
4. **Serve** – Serve with whipped cream and powdered sugar.

Lemon Ricotta Waffles

Ingredients:

- 1 ¾ cups all-purpose flour
- 1 tbsp sugar
- 1 tbsp baking powder
- ¼ tsp salt
- 2 eggs
- 1 cup ricotta cheese
- 1 cup milk
- ¼ cup melted butter
- 1 tbsp lemon zest
- 1 tsp vanilla extract

Instructions:

1. **Prepare batter** – Mix dry ingredients. In another bowl, whisk eggs, ricotta, milk, butter, lemon zest, and vanilla.
2. **Combine** – Stir wet ingredients into dry.
3. **Cook waffles** – Cook in a waffle iron until golden brown.
4. **Serve** – Serve with fresh berries and honey.

Matcha Mochi Waffles

Ingredients:

- 1 cup glutinous rice flour
- ½ cup all-purpose flour
- 2 tbsp sugar
- 1 tbsp matcha powder
- 1 tsp baking powder
- ¼ tsp salt
- 1 cup coconut milk
- 2 eggs
- ¼ cup melted butter
- 1 tsp vanilla extract

Instructions:

1. **Prepare batter** – Mix dry ingredients in one bowl and wet ingredients in another.
2. **Combine** – Stir wet ingredients into dry until smooth.
3. **Cook waffles** – Cook in a preheated waffle iron until crispy.
4. **Serve** – Serve with sweet red bean paste or condensed milk.

Red Velvet Waffles

Ingredients:

- 1 ½ cups all-purpose flour
- 2 tbsp cocoa powder
- ¼ cup sugar
- 1 tbsp baking powder
- ½ tsp salt
- 1 ½ cups buttermilk
- 2 eggs
- ¼ cup melted butter
- 1 tsp vanilla extract
- 1 tbsp red food coloring

For Cream Cheese Drizzle:

- 4 oz cream cheese, softened
- ½ cup powdered sugar
- 2 tbsp milk
- ½ tsp vanilla extract

Instructions:

1. **Prepare batter** – Whisk dry ingredients in a bowl. In another bowl, mix buttermilk, eggs, butter, vanilla, and food coloring.
2. **Combine** – Stir wet ingredients into dry until just combined.
3. **Cook waffles** – Pour batter into a preheated waffle iron and cook until crisp.
4. **Make glaze** – Whisk together cream cheese, powdered sugar, milk, and vanilla until smooth.
5. **Serve** – Drizzle with cream cheese glaze and serve warm.

Peanut Butter Banana Waffles

Ingredients:

- 1 ½ cups all-purpose flour
- 1 tbsp sugar
- 1 tsp baking powder
- ½ tsp baking soda
- ¼ tsp salt
- 1 ripe banana, mashed
- ½ cup peanut butter
- 1 ½ cups milk
- 2 eggs
- 1 tsp vanilla extract

Instructions:

1. **Prepare batter** – Whisk dry ingredients in one bowl. In another, mix banana, peanut butter, milk, eggs, and vanilla.
2. **Combine** – Stir wet ingredients into dry until smooth.
3. **Cook waffles** – Cook in a waffle iron until golden brown.
4. **Serve** – Serve with sliced bananas, honey, or extra peanut butter.

S'mores Waffles with Marshmallow Drizzle

Ingredients:

- 1 ½ cups all-purpose flour
- ¼ cup cocoa powder
- ¼ cup crushed graham crackers
- 1 tbsp sugar
- 1 tsp baking powder
- ½ tsp salt
- 1 ½ cups milk
- 2 eggs
- ¼ cup melted butter
- 1 tsp vanilla extract
- ½ cup mini chocolate chips

For Marshmallow Drizzle:

- ½ cup marshmallow fluff
- 2 tbsp milk

Instructions:

1. **Prepare batter** – Mix dry ingredients in one bowl. In another, whisk milk, eggs, butter, and vanilla.
2. **Combine** – Stir wet ingredients into dry, then fold in chocolate chips.
3. **Cook waffles** – Cook in a waffle iron until crispy.
4. **Make drizzle** – Heat marshmallow fluff with milk until smooth.
5. **Serve** – Drizzle marshmallow sauce over waffles and sprinkle with extra graham cracker crumbs.

Maple Bacon Waffles

Ingredients:

- 1 ½ cups all-purpose flour
- 1 tbsp sugar
- 1 tbsp baking powder
- ½ tsp salt
- 1 ¼ cups milk
- 2 eggs
- ¼ cup melted butter
- ½ cup cooked bacon, crumbled
- 1 tsp vanilla extract
- 2 tbsp maple syrup

Instructions:

1. **Prepare batter** – Mix dry ingredients. In another bowl, whisk milk, eggs, butter, vanilla, and maple syrup.
2. **Combine** – Stir wet ingredients into dry, then fold in crumbled bacon.
3. **Cook waffles** – Cook in a waffle iron until golden brown.
4. **Serve** – Serve with extra maple syrup and crispy bacon.

Apple Cider Waffles

Ingredients:

- 1 ¾ cups all-purpose flour
- 2 tbsp sugar
- 1 tbsp baking powder
- ½ tsp cinnamon
- ¼ tsp nutmeg
- ¼ tsp salt
- 1 cup apple cider
- ½ cup milk
- 2 eggs
- ¼ cup melted butter
- 1 tsp vanilla extract

Instructions:

1. **Prepare batter** – Mix dry ingredients in one bowl. In another, whisk apple cider, milk, eggs, butter, and vanilla.
2. **Combine** – Stir wet ingredients into dry until smooth.
3. **Cook waffles** – Cook in a waffle iron until crispy.
4. **Serve** – Serve with warm spiced apples or maple syrup.

Carrot Cake Waffles with Cream Cheese Glaze

Ingredients:

- 1 ½ cups all-purpose flour
- 1 tbsp brown sugar
- 1 tsp baking powder
- ½ tsp baking soda
- 1 tsp cinnamon
- ¼ tsp nutmeg
- ¼ tsp salt
- 1 cup buttermilk
- 2 eggs
- ¼ cup melted butter
- 1 tsp vanilla extract
- ½ cup grated carrots
- ¼ cup chopped walnuts (optional)

For Cream Cheese Glaze:

- 4 oz cream cheese, softened
- ½ cup powdered sugar
- 2 tbsp milk
- ½ tsp vanilla extract

Instructions:

1. **Prepare batter** – Mix dry ingredients in a bowl. In another, whisk buttermilk, eggs, butter, and vanilla.
2. **Combine** – Stir wet ingredients into dry, then fold in carrots and walnuts.
3. **Cook waffles** – Cook in a waffle iron until golden.
4. **Make glaze** – Whisk together cream cheese, powdered sugar, milk, and vanilla.
5. **Serve** – Drizzle cream cheese glaze over waffles and enjoy.

Coconut Flour Keto Waffles

Ingredients:

- ½ cup coconut flour
- 1 tsp baking powder
- ¼ tsp salt
- 4 eggs
- ½ cup almond milk
- 2 tbsp melted butter or coconut oil
- 1 tsp vanilla extract
- 1 tbsp granulated erythritol (or sweetener of choice)

Instructions:

1. **Prepare batter** – Mix dry ingredients in one bowl. In another, whisk eggs, almond milk, butter, vanilla, and sweetener.
2. **Combine** – Stir wet ingredients into dry until smooth.
3. **Cook waffles** – Cook in a waffle iron until golden.
4. **Serve** – Serve with sugar-free syrup or fresh berries.

Blueberry Cornmeal Waffles

Ingredients:

- 1 cup all-purpose flour
- ½ cup cornmeal
- 2 tbsp sugar
- 1 tbsp baking powder
- ½ tsp salt
- 1 ¼ cups buttermilk
- 2 eggs
- ¼ cup melted butter
- 1 tsp vanilla extract
- 1 cup fresh blueberries

Instructions:

1. **Prepare batter** – Mix dry ingredients in one bowl. In another, whisk buttermilk, eggs, butter, and vanilla.
2. **Combine** – Stir wet ingredients into dry, then gently fold in blueberries.
3. **Cook waffles** – Cook in a waffle iron until golden and crisp.
4. **Serve** – Serve with maple syrup and extra blueberries.

Gingerbread Waffles

Ingredients:

- 1 ¾ cups all-purpose flour
- ¼ cup brown sugar
- 1 tbsp baking powder
- 1 tsp cinnamon
- 1 tsp ground ginger
- ¼ tsp nutmeg
- ¼ tsp salt
- 1 ¼ cups milk
- 2 eggs
- ¼ cup molasses
- ¼ cup melted butter
- 1 tsp vanilla extract

Instructions:

1. **Prepare batter** – Mix dry ingredients in a bowl. In another, whisk milk, eggs, molasses, butter, and vanilla.
2. **Combine** – Stir wet ingredients into dry until smooth.
3. **Cook waffles** – Cook in a preheated waffle iron until crisp.
4. **Serve** – Serve with whipped cream and a dusting of powdered sugar.

Taro Ube Waffles

Ingredients:

- 1 ½ cups all-purpose flour
- 2 tbsp sugar
- 1 tbsp baking powder
- ½ tsp salt
- 1 cup ube or taro puree
- 1 cup coconut milk
- 2 eggs
- ¼ cup melted butter
- 1 tsp vanilla extract

Instructions:

1. **Prepare batter** – Mix dry ingredients in one bowl. In another, whisk ube/taro puree, coconut milk, eggs, butter, and vanilla.
2. **Combine** – Stir wet ingredients into dry until smooth.
3. **Cook waffles** – Cook in a waffle iron until golden.
4. **Serve** – Serve with condensed milk drizzle or coconut flakes.

Mocha Espresso Waffles

Ingredients:

- 1 ½ cups all-purpose flour
- ¼ cup cocoa powder
- ¼ cup sugar
- 1 tbsp baking powder
- 1 tsp instant espresso powder
- ½ tsp salt
- 1 ¼ cups milk
- 2 eggs
- ¼ cup melted butter
- 1 tsp vanilla extract

Instructions:

1. **Prepare batter** – Mix dry ingredients in one bowl. In another, whisk milk, eggs, butter, and vanilla.
2. **Combine** – Stir wet ingredients into dry until just mixed.
3. **Cook waffles** – Cook in a preheated waffle iron until crisp.
4. **Serve** – Serve with chocolate sauce and whipped cream.

Bourbon Pecan Waffles

Ingredients:

- 1 ½ cups all-purpose flour
- 2 tbsp brown sugar
- 1 tbsp baking powder
- ½ tsp salt
- 1 ¼ cups milk
- ¼ cup bourbon
- 2 eggs
- ¼ cup melted butter
- ½ cup chopped pecans

Instructions:

1. **Prepare batter** – Mix dry ingredients in a bowl. In another, whisk milk, bourbon, eggs, and butter.
2. **Combine** – Stir wet ingredients into dry, then fold in pecans.
3. **Cook waffles** – Cook in a waffle iron until golden.
4. **Serve** – Serve with warm maple syrup and extra pecans.

Honey Butter Sweet Potato Waffles

Ingredients:

- 1 cup mashed sweet potato
- 1 ½ cups all-purpose flour
- 2 tbsp sugar
- 1 tbsp baking powder
- ½ tsp cinnamon
- ¼ tsp nutmeg
- ¼ tsp salt
- 1 ¼ cups buttermilk
- 2 eggs
- ¼ cup melted butter
- 1 tsp vanilla extract

For Honey Butter:

- ¼ cup butter, softened
- 2 tbsp honey

Instructions:

1. **Prepare batter** – Mix dry ingredients in one bowl. In another, whisk sweet potato, buttermilk, eggs, butter, and vanilla.
2. **Combine** – Stir wet ingredients into dry until smooth.
3. **Cook waffles** – Cook in a waffle iron until golden.
4. **Make honey butter** – Mix softened butter and honey.
5. **Serve** – Spread honey butter over warm waffles.

Raspberry Almond Waffles

Ingredients:

- 1 ½ cups all-purpose flour
- 2 tbsp sugar
- 1 tbsp baking powder
- ½ tsp salt
- 1 cup milk
- 2 eggs
- ¼ cup melted butter
- ½ cup fresh raspberries
- ¼ cup sliced almonds
- 1 tsp almond extract

Instructions:

1. **Prepare batter** – Mix dry ingredients in one bowl. In another, whisk milk, eggs, butter, and almond extract.
2. **Combine** – Stir wet ingredients into dry, then fold in raspberries and almonds.
3. **Cook waffles** – Cook in a waffle iron until crisp.
4. **Serve** – Serve with raspberry sauce or powdered sugar.

Chocolate-Stuffed Waffles

Ingredients:

- 1 ½ cups all-purpose flour
- 2 tbsp sugar
- 1 tbsp baking powder
- ½ tsp salt
- 1 ¼ cups milk
- 2 eggs
- ¼ cup melted butter
- ½ cup chocolate chips or chocolate spread

Instructions:

1. **Prepare batter** – Mix dry ingredients in one bowl. In another, whisk milk, eggs, and butter.
2. **Cook waffles** – Pour half of the batter into a preheated waffle iron. Add chocolate chips or a spoonful of chocolate spread, then cover with more batter.
3. **Finish cooking** – Close the waffle iron and cook until crispy.
4. **Serve** – Dust with powdered sugar and enjoy warm.

www.ingramcontent.com/pod-product-compliance
Lightning Source LLC
LaVergne TN
LVHW081506060526
838201LV00056BA/2957